Two Books

by Larry G. Bierman

Shake My Faith, Kiss This

∞∞

So Longing Goes On

Written with the sponsorship of the
Contemporary Arts Foundation,
Oklahoma City, Oklahoma

Two Books: Shake My Faith, Kiss This
& So Longing Goes On © 1974, 1977
and 2010 by Larry G. Bierman

Cover and Book design by Larry G Bierman

All rights reserved. The use of any part of this publication through any means, electronic, recording, print, or otherwise, without prior consent of the publisher is an infringement of the copyright laws. The only exception is by reviewer, who may quote short excerpts in a review or article.

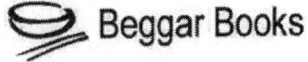 Beggar Books

Published by BeggarBooks.com
310 Keith
Norman, Oklahoma 73069

Contents

Book One	1
The Artist	2
Shake My Faith, Kiss This	3
Dedication Page	4
Introduction by Mike Mullin	5
You lay on the cold floor	6
#1 So far	7
Riding on a Bus	8
The Desert Birds Drunk Burgundy	10
Boots & Vi	11
The Letter	12
Franks's Dedication	13
Things to Do in a Rain Pour	14
Blue Mountain Essay #1	16
Bill:	18
Frank!	19
Statement	20
So Far / Boas	21
While Vi Reads Her Bible	22
Early Death	23
King a Hard Bottles	24
Ms. Wednesday Night, June '68	26
Chet—	27
I'd Swear It Was the Jukebox	28
La Plaza	29
A 6,000 Year Old Love	30
Check List / Hamburger Blues	31
Gleaming Points	32
Phone-Booth Blues	34

DOWN POURS: / The CIA	35
More Things to Do in a Rain Pour	36
Joel's Song	38
Café Sparkin'	40
Monday, April 23, '68	41
Kontakion	42
Hear the Beautiful Cow	44
Mobile Alabama Mobile-Home	45
Dirk & Flow	46
Things to Buy / For Flow's Diary	48
Blue Mountain Incident	49
Chet Was Singing—I Was Dreaming	52
Sincerely Lonely	53
Too Much Was What It Was	56
I Had Terrible Paper	57
Chet Wrote This One	58
The *Cold Wave* Series	60
Bill's Beautiful Call	61
Frank Made This Up for Us	63
The Last We Ever Heard	64
Full Moon through the Veranda Door	65
I'll Meet You Tonight	66
A Face of Excitement	68
Good Lookin'	70
Weird Clouds / Fortune Cookie	71
It's Tough Being Tough	73
Of the Author	75
Book Two	77
So Longing Goes On	79
I am Fire	80
Burgers in Bed	83
	85

Heart Jewels	86
OPAL / Missing Part	87
Breakfast News	88
Carl's Vietnam Death	89
SO LONGING GOES ON	90
Reincarnate	91
AM-FM	92
A Headband Construction/Journal Entry	93
Let a Lot	94
Long Long Haul	95
Innocent So/Wow	96
Tulsa Speedway:	97
LIF/No Joke, Joe	98
Buffalo, Oklahoma	99
Braniff-Flight 980	100
Longing	101
Look Up Words / 6:45 Arrival	102
Cone	103
Snowman*in*Moonlight / Appeal	104
Power Glide / Standing Looking	105
HELL / EAT-YOUR $	106
Drawing to Color (Denver, Colorado)	107
want/to want	108
First Lessons in Food & Drink	109
Meditate	110
Ponca City Birth	111
Light above Table / NOTH	112
Six on the Last Straw / A V	113
Dropping like Flies	114
Flown the Coop	115
Last Will	116

Dance by Yourself	117
For Christy	118
Guitar Music	119
Showed *(for Nick Sunday)*	120
Is Your Soul Worth 25¢?	121
Hold Up / "Wh	122
Got Kicked Out Of School	123
Watched the Marquee Change/@	124
Relax-It	125
Tag	126
Wonder Why Wonder	127
Thick Covers on the Lamp/Drinks	128
Camp Night-Meet	129
Durant Tour	130
Word Workers of the World, Unite!	132
Cozy	133
KATT	134
February / Of Coors	135
Hush Up	136
Sonic Drive-in	137
Airbrushed Bushes / Go Up	138
I See / Tightly Packed Deck	139
From the Girl that Could not Be/Aside	140
Ginger Lake Lady	141
Mutt Street	142
Glib Future	143
I'm Your Slave, Joe / The Grapes / There're	144
2:00AM on the Band Bus	145
Woman in Dark Brown	146
Smoke Escapes	147
O	148

You Don't Have to be Broke	149
STR / Suspect	150
Best Mistake / Favorite Stains	151
Sky Bottle / Hobby Boy	152
Pull the Birds off Doorknobs	153
If You've Love/Gone from Us Now	154
Blues Mountain	155
All Guy Said Was / Leop'ard	156
Oh. God	157
Bum-a-Stamp / Certain	158
Soon as Can Be / Sobre Solo	159
Romance	160
Please Me	161
Bad Dog	163
Detroit Dues—Waltz	164
Bar Talk / One Name Less	165
Belief to Believe	166
Hard / Bound	167
Word Worker	169
Love Poem	170
Let Me Now	171
(Alter Ego)	172

"There is no fire like passion,
  there is no shark like hatred,
  there is no snare like folly,
  there is no torrent like greed."
    —Siddhartha Gautame Buddha

Introduction

After thirty-five years I am happy to issue a combined new edition of my first two books. *Shake My Faith, Kiss This / So Longing Goes On.* The original books were printed in south Oklahoma City in editions of 500 copies.

Printed as part of a series of books sponsored by J.R. Witt and the Contemporary Arts Foundation. The CAF was the center of new poetry, art and sculpture, as well as new play production. The CAF included studios, gallery space, a theater and, at one time, a foundry. Sunday poetry readings were a regular event and J. R. managed to make sure there was a good spread of fruit, cheese, and, bless him, a "gentle" wine.

All this was much appreciated by the young actors, artists and poets in the neighborhood. This was often the best meal they would have all week. J.R. understood what is truly important. I was impressed that he knew Kenneth Patchen. My love for J. R. and his wife Fran grows even though they are gone.

Odd to think that I am now as old as J. R. was when he captained the CAF crew.

Tragically, the CAF was destroyed by fire—the Jamie Barnes gallery and all the artwork stored there, the studios, the stage, and many copies of CAF books were lost—golden age ended in ash.

The first layouts were done using press-on letters, 8x10 index cards, a Royal Standard manual, and rubber cement. This new edition holds closely to the old layouts. I have made changes taking advantage of computer technology. A few of the old layout pages are scanned in and used to give a little of the original funk.

I have changed a few of the poems, but not by much, corrected some misspelled words, added punctuation here and there, and arranged some of the poems to better fit the page.

The title type is Bookman Old Style bold; the poems are in Times New Roman 12 pt. My idea is to set the poems so that old, tired eyes can see them.

      Enjoy!

              Larry G. Bierman
              Summer, 2010
              Norman, Oklahoma

Book One

Shake My Faith,

Kiss This

My love: Mike. John.
Thanx to J. R. [and thanks all
you who were so patient with me
while this book was being born.
  Especially:
    *Mr. Flight Control
    *Nancy, I don't mean to
      shock you. XOXOX
    *Tom, yes, I mean it. Yes.

  And to the silent one . . .
    (you know who you are)
      my entire faith.

        LG
  Oklahoma, April '74

PS: Mistakes are unfortunate.

Introduction

all weekend
we have needed
some lipstick --
throughout this
book the places
where the lipstick
blots are missing
is where they
should be --
(ladies, please
feel free
to kiss this book
anywhere you
feel free

kiss me quick

Mike Mullin

You lay on the cold floor
and shuffle a deck of cards.
You listen while someone upstairs
learns to play the electric guitar.
You feel for your stomach.
You realize, of course,
that the game's been called off.
You cut the deck
—an ace of clubs.
You rub your fingernails
against your shirt.

Your hear someone say,
"Oh, I forgot something."
& the door slams again.

———

Frank says, "Look, I don't really care
　　what your name is."

———

We don't have time to blow.
We barely have time to sneeze.
　　　　　　—Jim

#1.
So far
We've come
This far,
Now we
Only have
So far
To go…

Riding on a Bus

Riding on a bus,
I don't know where I'm going. Just
riding on a bus
up through the pine tree forest
into mountain air,
a little brown boy
has a big blue basket,
and the rooster inside
is crowing fantastic.
The rooster inside is
crowing—cock-a-doodle.

Riding on a bus,
over narrow bridges
and glimmering rivers,
riding on a bus,
going to the centers
of commercial interest,
a little brown boy
in a green serape
takes his rooster to the market
for some money.
The rooster in the basket
crows, oh—cock-a-doodle.

Riding on a bus
there is a gold Madonna
and a bent antenna.
Riding on a bus,
the driver hums along
with the radio's song,
while a little brown boy
in a white sombrero
folds his hands and
says a simple prayer for
the pale red rooster
crowing—cock-a-doodle.

The Desert Birds Drunk Burgundy

We work so, so hard all summer,
Miss Lena and Me.
We work so hard just to stain
    the living room wine—
we don't have time to blow.

Miss Lena keeps the goblets full
    and brings the flowers.
I can almost reach into the corners
    with a long gladiolus.
My snot is dripping on the rug.

Lena's authentic Comanche weaving.
Well, I tell her, we should
    just roll it up out of the path.
But she has this fear of moving
    shoeless on bare floors.
She says it makes her ankles prickle.

Boots & Vi

The Letter

Vi—
I used to roll in the streets.
And.
While I had a little brass pipe.
I used to take baths in mercury
　　light.
But.
Though I'm seldom by myself.
I used to preten' affection for
　　you, love.
I used to roll into that hotel.
Yes.
There was dusk on the balcony.
I used to could dance and
　　danced all night.
No.
Even if the danger has grown.
I refused to pretend.
　　　Love,
　　　　　Boots

THIS BOOK IS DEDICATED TO JIM,
who is hiding out
in the mountains.

THIS BOOK IS DEDICATED TO HIM

—Frank

Things to Do in a Rain Pour

There's the busy signal
so you look out the window.
You listen to you lips in a rain pour.
The radio, steps and a squeaky door
are things you can hear in a rainstorm.
In a downpour you rub your eyes,
scratch under your arm and yawn.
The window has to be closed.
You blow dust off a book.
You find an old mystery novel.
A yellow letter is discovered.
You fold a paper airplane
and decide to write a relative.
You plan to use some wood glue.
You eat a spoonful of lemon Jell-O;
take down a can of soup and leave it.
Pour you some more coffee.
There's a centipede that evening.
You put another quilt on the couch.
There's yourself in the bathroom mirror.
You take your temperature for no reason,
itch your teeth and with fingernails.

You turn on the television without sound.
You sneeze and there's a ricochet.
You set another pan in the floor
and kick it by accident.
You limp and light a candle.
You make plans for another vacation.

The ache in your knee acts up.
Someone has some liquor.
You scribble on the cover of a quarterly.
One person crochets,
another thumbs through PLAYBOY.
You hold a velvet pillow in your lap
and comb your hair with a toothpick.
You eat most of the gumdrops
while trying to balance your checkbook.
You take your shower early.
You blow your nose and it thunders.
The wind sounds mean, so
you take a warm shower.
You put on your slippers and robe.
The phone is a wrong number.
You stand in the doorway.

Blue Mountain Essay #1

a. They're beautiful
   Cream-colored moccasins
   and they're on sale
   @ 20% off.

b. One way or another
   don't we all fall in love.
   Ain't it more common
   than the common cold.

c. Influenza can influence ya.
   You have some choices.
   Which do you choose:
   convenience or Paris? (Caprice?)

d. At one time or other
   doesn't love get too serious
   to keep it under covers?
   Don't you have to say it?

e. The white man was eating
   his second glass eye.
   This was not his own
   This one was Irish.

f. Some choices force us:
   P.S.*
   Jump the fence,
   or miss the short cut.

g. Frank thinks, "if I were
   a little more intelligent
   I would probably be bored—
   I can't stand this loll."

*Expect a detour—
   if not a dead end.

Bill:

There are probably potatoes
under the sink.
If you boil them first
you will be able to eat them.

Be sure to unplug the coffee
before you go to work.
It still needs to be fixed.

Aunt Luella said she
might come by Sunday
to pick up her dress.
I put it in the closet
in the hall.
It still needs buttons.

There is money in the cookie jar
for the paperboy
when he comes for it.
Be sure to keep the receipt.

I won't be back this week.
If you need me I'll call.

Frank!

"I love you," but he doesn't mean it.
"...certainly sprouts under the spigot."
—Mark

Statement

Frank says, "I'm not going
    to say anything."

All my glances turned
toward your silence.
I love you. An
understatement, I love
you.

I wake up. There is
nothing immediate.
It is always the morning
before or after—
I need you. Think of
yourself. I need you.

The day almost as dark as
night, soon.
I hope what light is left
will not quit—
in the window marbles in
a jar and
    your photograph.

So Far

We've come
This far,
Now we
Only have
So far
To Go
Stop me
Next time
You get
A chance…
The chance.

Boas

When you move me
please be careful
with my Audubon
feather collection.
This morning in bed
and clinging to
the window sill,
like to the side
of an overturned
kayak, I worry
about you
and my collection.

While Vi Reads Her Bible

Frank is in the kitchen
with his science fiction.
Dirk is on the patio
with his guitar and radio.
Chet is in the bedroom
meditating like his guru.
Joel is in the cellar
working the garage sale.

The house is full of card tables.

Frank said, "Far as I can tell
we're either living spiritual
or we're living very minimal."
As usual, Boots' only interest
is his own survival.

Eugene died
in the Tahitian hills.
Rumor has it
she's doing swell.

Her things are on the table,
her kimono, her fan and her rifle.

Early Death

Frank says, "I had a friend who did commit
suicide.

One morning his mother
called him down to breakfast
and in just a little bit

        she heard a gun go off.

                They buried
                him the next
                      day."

King a Hard Bottles

and don't know
or didn't you
surely you was
saw that guy there
you call him Dusty
write that all out
lay words on sheets
did you know good
that grave gave way
ol' hair snag tree
and didn't you shuffle
a whole damn school
wasn't your feet off
in that there vacancy
that broken stage
or didn't big black
heard crows echo echo
echo back like that
sure don't shit if
and book eyes torn
rip out so sadly

then sheet music look
read this rusty cloud
them colors worry
those water bother us
dear lord
        juggle me

such many thin legs
these mark of knees
don't you feel for
and are knees of love?

King a Hard Bottles
give the flavors of
and scrumptious yes
better and moon melon
better and lake water

weren't we together
you there and Dusty
me? I can't tell by

damn the burnt coffee

Ms. Wednesday Night, June '68

Eggs bounce in some boiling water.
Beer sounds on the radio,
the rainstorms & some drizzle
come down round your pretty ears.
Frizzy lights on flurry weaving's,
Mouths that liquor into the dim,
at the window bamboo clusters.
Amusement gathers in your arms.
I sink into the kitchen sofa
as weather peels the paper down.
Lip my smoke & breathe in softly.
It is welcome as a hug.
Don't feel me like a stranger.
Don't fear you'll misunderstand.
This is just my personal language,
so lay back comfy hold my hands.
We rest us on this satin comfort
as peals of weather come thunder down.
You're such a friend to have emotions.
You're such a woman to help a man.

"I don't want <u>to hurt the d</u>irt anymore."
  —Dirk

Chet—

How was the party?
Was it a party?
Were there more people there
than I would imagine?
Did they all get trashed?
Did they get it all picked up?
You were there.
Weren't you there?
I would've come,
but I was alone.
I mean I was off
by myself.
It's been beautiful.
The party must have
been a riot.
Did anyone miss me?

Well, did I miss much?

    Yours,
           June

I'd Swear It Was the Jukebox but It May Have Been the Beer

I was talkin' to a gal you know,
and she is a friend of mine.
She told me that she loves you
but to her love you're blind.
She told me how you thrill her.
She wants you night and day,
and she said how it hurts her
the way you stay away.
But if you ask her now
she'll say, "I'm doin' fine."
Only, man, let me tell you
I've seen her, seen her cryin'.

I ain't speakin' any names, now.
You know who I talk about,
but let me tell you what she told me—
think it's time and you found out.
She tol' me, and she was drinkin',
she said, "he drives me wild."
Then she leaned against my shoulder
and she shook just like a child.
But if you ask her now
she'll say, "I'm doin' fine."
Only, man, let me tell you,
I've heard her, heard her cryin'.

Maybe you don't love her.
You might not even care,
but let me say she's a woman
and a kind that's always rare.
And let me tell you, she told me,
she said, "I love him, sure, it's real."
Now, when it comes to love, boy,
you won't find a better deal.
But if you ask her now
she'll smile, "I'm doin' fine."
Only, brother, let me tell you,
I've heard her, I've seen her cry.

La Plaza

If parrots
were the same
as balloons,
and they are,

we could watch
hotdogs fly
around the cathe-
dral—we do.

*Who said I wrote this
  a long time ago?*

Well, they lied.

A 6,000 Year Old Love

The rocks suddenly grow larger.
I feel them in my hands.
I feel the rocks grown large,
rocks weighing in my hands.

I cannot move my hands.
I cannot hold my hands.
I cannot hold my hands
and the dark is black.

You help me hold my arms.
The air is suddenly quieter.
You help me hold my hands.
Quietly, the moon grows larger.

Check List

Pick yr teeth.
Pick them ticks
    outta yr arm pits.
Scratch where
    chiggers itch.
Put a little spit
    where the wasp hit.
It's a field trip.
Don't be sick.

Hamburger Blues

Since you broke my heart
I've had no one, baby,
to melt my cheese
or to keep the onions
from makin' me cry.

Gleaming Points

Rusted nails in old paint pails.
Galvanized washtub full of snails.
Folks eatin' oysters on the half shell.
Those black men throwing dice with knives.
Generous slices of onion and cucumber.
Wives burning off bunions—off their heels.
With diamond matches—off their heels.
Kids acting smart in their pa's new Ford.
An old woman playing an ancient guitar.
Pink, rose covered doilies. Mahogany.
Windowpanes with lace and waves.
Then an ugly face. Somebody else's.
A vase arranged with bright red dahlias.
This oil can in a greasy vice. Begonias.
Someone dropping a chunk of ice.
Goose pimples on a sun burnt back.
A host of beds and spooks at night.
Shivering under a single sheet in quiet.
A body. A lady. A lover. The covers.
The lake full of dancing larva.

A washstand and a bar of Lava.
Frank working on his next novel.
His next, he's sure will win the Nobel.
Women in chins and white chairs. Beers.
Stick men on bridges. More snails.
A train loaded with guns for sell.
Someone in the window who waves.
The rippled glass and the shutters.
Two youths in a fatal crash.
Mashed potatoes on a blue willow plate.
Chet in his transcendent state. Fate.
Ma's hoe handle on a chicken neck.

A snake. The rake. The coiled water hose.
A boy playing dead by the caved in sewer.
The half finished storm cellar. Sea Salt.
All rotten fence posts at a proper slant.
Chills going down her skinny spine.
A sound made in rabbit wire. A ghost.
A baseball card with Mickey Mantle's weight.
Fat mama stewin' down at the lodge.
White girls riding a pretty barge.
A college degree.

The family tree.

Anyone of the Kennedy's.

A transplant.
A total flop.
Red clay pots in floral foil.
A sling shot. The ordinary rock.
Dirt on the carpet and the dahlias.
A bouquet of ostrich plumes and such.
Canned plums from the county fair.
An invalid spinster screaming "Stop!"
Waiting on a certain envelope.
Waiting on a package tied with rope.
Aluminum wrappers on the
                linoleum floor.

A piece of metallic tile.
The candle.
      The points.
            Gleaming.

Phone-Booth Blues

Lipstick blotted on his collar.
Numbers scribbled on a dollar.
He dials the phone, midnight caller,
mad that she won't let him ball her.

DOWN POURS: Another Episode from the Blue Mountains.

Frank: I been in love
    all week.

Lena: I know
    how it feels.

Frank: Oh, it has nothing
    to do with you.

Lena: I know. I said,
    I know how
        it feels.

The CIA

There is after all
nothing certain about
being evasive.

More Things to Do in a Rain Pour

Smoke a cigarette.
Learn to play Monopoly solitaire.
Draw angels in a matchbook.
You can carve dolls out of sponge.
Think about the light on the walls.
There's a car that's out of breaks.
You can staple pages together
    at all four corners.

Open drawers and close drawers.
Look for something without
    knowing what.
Wait around for the newspaper to
    use.

Pretend your fingers are Ginger Rogers.
You can recall a collage.
You can converse with a moth
    and not move your mouth.

There's a spider crossing the ceiling.
Just the way the centipede went.
You don't move your lips.
You can rearrange your rose rocks.

Wish for a yard full of blue spruce.
You can pick your preferred profile.
You can play with a piece of
    masking tape.

Make a loop around your finger
    and stick it to your nose.

You can massage the heel of your hand.
You can practice a new dance step.
You're going to call this one—
                Tarantella.

Do you ever think of spiders as
    being passionate?
        Centipedes?
Remember when it rained
    four years ago.
You can get up early
        and go back to bed.
You can bend a paperclip
           into a spiral.
Empty all the ashtrays at least once.

Take a walk with your blue plastic
                  umbrella.
        You can hum.

Joel's Song

Don't
remind me
of you.
No, don't
whatever
you do.
I've been tryin'
so hard
to forget
that we ever
(did we ever)
ever met.
O, don't
remind me
  of you.

Don't
remind me
of the time
we laughed,
we slobbered
and wined.
You held me
held me tight,
'n said "I know
it's alright.
It's—
alright."
But don't
remind me
  of when.

You don't
remind me
of you.
Not the way
you used to.
It's true.
Glad times go past
fast as
the sad ones.
Guess it's best
we recall
no time at all.
Don't remind me
(what's the use)
of what we
  used
    to
Do.

—Imagine, if you will, a warm night in March, 1956. Joel and Colette are parked on the bank of the Red River somewhere near Lone Wolf, Oklahoma. Joel has his arm around Colette and he says something like this:

Café Sparkin'

Your face was fat and buttery as pancakes
this morning when the sun rubbed down on you.

Colette, tell me, how is your precious herb patch?
I saw you working it with sprinklers and a rake.

You remind me so much of ginger or nutmeg
I think about you with tea or in good eggnog.

The earth has turned, has turned, has been turned.
Colette, don't you remember who it was used you?

Let me pour down, Colette, like thick honey syrup
all over your cheek bones and beautiful elbows.

Aren't there seed packets in your sewing basket?
I thought I saw squash and okra, tomaters and peas.

Oklahoma's so far away…when you consider the stars.
And, Colette, I sure like to consider them with you.

Don't you think the moon's a powder-sugared
                                        flapjack?
Come on! let me lick the taste right out of your hair.

Monday, April 23, '68

Dear Fuckn' Frank.
                               I don't know. Was it a lie? I've gone broke. My eyes don't work. I can't trust what I hear. I don't know how. They just got broke. I let the wrong friends use them. I thought they were friends, I mean, were my friends. I guess that's where I blew it. What do you say? What's the use to say? Why can't I?

Why can't I hear you? I know now I got eyes. See the pretty water. It falls all around this letter. (They don't know what to make of it—the friendly ones and all their family lives. They make me want a blood bath in my own blood. Why?)

Why have you always been the younger?

God, I'm sorry I said that. I didn't mean to admit that. It's just that I can't understand. Why do you use your life in such a way? It makes mine seem so like a waste that I feel I need help? What do they call help? The way you push me away? The way I avoid you so you don't get the chance? What's hope?

Guess it's only me. Guess I never tried, but somehow I've always wanted to be you. I know how far that is to reach. Hell, nobody taught me anything without pains. And you've taught me more than anyone. It hurts to be without you. It hurts not having a reason to be with you.

But DON'T GET SCARED. I'm not asking for…

I don't know what to ask for.
                    Your fuckn' bro,
                              Jim

Kontakion

The only connection between us
*   is this prayer.*

I.   This morning.
      This.
      Knots on a page.
      A diagram.
      High lies again.

II. His warming.
      His.
      Lock on a barge.
      The diamond.
      In time for them.

III. Kiss imploring
      kiss.
      What's in a word?
      The dimming of a friend.
      No one knows when.

V. These mornings.
   This.
   Shouts in a crowd.
   Long Island sound.
   The chime times ten.

VI. She's warning.
    Hiss.
    Shouts and reward.
    He tries and
    his skin gives in.

VII. Bless forming
     bliss.
     Hurts in a rage.
     Hearts by the pound.
     Feel steel still.
     Again.

        Again.

Hear the Beautiful Cow

I look out at the windmill for the lemon sun,
the bitter shine light the color of wheat fields.
I go out the door for a walk to the hills,
have pulled myself up out of a chair and gone.

I ride my boots over the mud-covered knolls.
My heels slide on the rocks on the rutted path
that all the horses seem to follow anymore,
though I seldom hear their clop clop behind me.

Inside the Scrub blackbirds caw as I ford
the creek. I've hiked once more from Bell Cow
to the one called Wild Horse. Hiked on home.
I lean on the porch post and grin. Just listen.

Mobile Alabama Mobile-Home

Tonight is a good night
          for pineapple.
We can have a table cloth.
Tonight is a good night
   for listening to Debussy
      and the air conditioner.
We can string the paper lanterns.
Tonight is a good night
   for simple tastes.

You can tell about how water
   is a far out kind of substance.
Tonight is a good night
    for us to hold hands and kiss.
I've made a list of things
    it'd be nice for us to do.
I suspect they'll get done
    without the use of it.

Dirk & Flow

Dirk: Hey.

(There's a commotion on the stairs.)

Frank: Hello? Hello?

Dirk: Hunh?

Frank (comes in the door): It's just me.

Dirk: Hey.

Frank: Well?

Dirk: Nothing. I just wanted to know who it was.

Frank: Just me. I got some rice.

Dirk: Okay?

Frank (puts the sack on the drain board): And I got some peanut butter and bread, in case you want any... got beer too. You want some?

Dirk: I had breakfasts already.

Attention plus que 5 feuilles de SUP-AIR

Things to Buy

1. box of cornflakes
2. two faced shaving mirror
3. magnifying glass
4. vanilla candles
5.

For Flow's Diary, 2/20/72

A smile is free—is all—is enough.
I give you lips. You give them—yours.
A circle of friends is—close—as love.
A smile is all—is at least—enough.

Frank: There's something about the
feel of France'll make your
fingers smell funny.

Blue Mountain Incident

1. The Move, the Midnight & Who

Make a thin white line,
draw it out on your knuckles.
They shout your name, Boots.
This is the only reason
you glance up in time.
A ten ton blue mirror
hangs high above your face.
This is the real reason
locks are kept on the attic,
a dotted line on the scalp.
And if you're not cautious
a trough of water on the walk
can be dangerous and deep
as any open well. You stop
for a startle and fall cold
at the murderer's furious lisp.

* * *

Was it Mary, the murderer's gal?
The fumes up around her throat
the sound of their disagreements,
the pressure of his thumbs
against the flesh and liquid of…

(Overheard by the stable)
'Don' tell them nothin'.
This's much secre-sí
An' maybe they's never
goin' guess what if."
"You no, nothin' yes?"
"I thin' yes. No, no
they's no guess, ever no."

2. —Here Come the Wranglers, &
   after those Rustlin' Wrestlers—

Get a hold of your straps, Boots.
Pull yourself up out of here.
Beer, take a swig and spit it.
Draw your line in the dust.
Do it with your big heel.
The more of aggravation
works your jaw muscles.
Draw it in the dirt and sawdust.
Ain't that a hot little lump in
your throat, fist, breeches?

   * * *

Nights! Nights of fever,
hollow fever of crowds
and all of them cowards.
The blue 'elirium lonesome.
O, the fervor of wounds.

    * * *

Move or you lose your
talent for equilibrium.
A man gotta eat steak,
drink liquors and laugh.
A man gotta get fucked
in range of riflers or not.
Scares the scars off me. Does.
No favor for killed, kid.
They said he always said
"gotta love'm where they live."

    * * *

Get it, then leave it.

    * * *

WATCH OUT!
                    Boots!?
The BAR—
Ten tons of blue go broke.
And your reflections roll
in the air like day old smoke.

Chet Was Singing—I Was Dreaming

blue
woman
come home
lean on me
say pretty
you're
pretty
pretty feet
nice
fingers
lovely

blue woman
write words
send them on
say lordy
pretty woman
beautiful girl
such soft arms
your long way
make dreams

blue woman
the dark time
dark time
on the party
line
soft pretty
lips
beautiful
face
such warm
eyes
make love
make me

Sincerely Lonely

Don't think.
Don't you think
you've been thinking
enough now?
Don't you think
it's high time
you took
that phone off
the hook
and gave me a ring?
Don't you think
you should say
what you think?
Don't you think?
What do you say?
Don't you think?
it's about time
you told your man
what's on you mind.
You've been thinking.
You've been up
late at night
thinking up
your cute lies.

You've been thinking
of calling us off.
I know your fingers.
I know how they
drum the counter
like a cheap bongo.
Don't get anxious.
But don't get anguished.
Just because I am.
What I'm telling you is this—
this is it.

If your mind's made up,
then say so.
You don't have to make up
a speech just for me.
Don't think about it—
don't for a split second.
Just blurt it now.
You have any second thought.
You've been thinking hard.
You've been trying to
read my mind
and thinking how hard
it is to tell it
Tell it like it is.
Just like this.

I can tell.

Okay.

Fine.

Things always work out
when you walk out.
No doubt.
Just pay them no mind.
The folks will take care
of the boys.
If you want to get away.
If you want to leave
and get things
out of your system.
Sort things out.
Think things through.
Maybe you should.
But don't worry.
Not for an instant.
I'll get along alone
somehow.

Dear.

PS. Damn you.

Johnny—
This year it's us, not you, who're presumptuous.
—Streaker

Too Much Was What It Was

Let's make the whole house
    smell like popcorn.
Let's put on a record
    and eat up a storm.
Let's go down south
    say, as far as Houston.
It's been a long time
    since we've been around
        each other down there.
It seems like a long time
    since the last pound, you
        knocking on the door.
It has been a long time
    but not as long as before.
Let's make more popcorn
    than the pan can handle.*
Let's spill popcorn
    on the floor.

*"We make 7 or 8 batches every night."
    —Steve

I Had Terrible Paper

Silence…I start out.
    ` It is a letter.
And it is a moment.
                      And it is this.
    Silence, I write in ink and with
  bitter coffee in a glass.
     I am so restless.
Silence in this effort. Is it all words?
I move my fingers and move
              them again.
                      Silence.
   This is a page of quiet work.
                 I draw words.
I move an old fountain pen.
   Silence,
      your presence intimidates me.
Unlike loud noise, it is all intimate.
Silence, hours on hours and all lovely
              in my thought.
        Nerves gone coma numb.
   I wait.
I put fingers on face.
            I feel a breath.
And here's where a kiss
          pours out…

Chet Wrote This One

Every day's a danger
with everybody's hand.
You got to keep yourself alone,
or you got to find a friend.
Put yourself in glasses.
Now look me in the eye.
Don't take away your love, boy,
or you'll have to watch me cry.

But don't let the beat fall—
But don't let it drop—
You got to keep your feet going,
Or you got to stop…

        Measures of sand.
        Drummers and pans.
        Smokers and plans.
        Holders and candles.
        Famous as angels.
        The women and the wind.
        Drinkers and cans.
        Dancers and friends.
        Singers and bands.
        Everyone stands.
        Or falls in the end
            Say it again—

Put yourself in my place.
Then do just what you please.
We got to be together,
so I say it on my knees—
But don't let the beat fail.
But don't let it drop.
You got to keep your feet going.
You got to keep what you got to.
You got to keep your feet going.
Or you got to stop.

Chet Foster

The *Cold Wave* Series

    1.
It's a silent dance we do
around the low and yellow candle.

I don't want to stand in your shoes.

Your arms are too much to handle.

What's love without excuse or
               reason?
We both wear sleeves long
            this season.

    2.
When this scares me I try
   to think about what dad
      always said about how,
         "even gold only glitters."
            —Jim

Bill's Beautiful Call

Say it in silence—
You spill the crayons.
You say as it pleases
here with the faces
in this crowded corral.

Say it more reverently—
Oh, grow your nails,
then bare your shins,
here where we wear
our jeans very thin.

Oh, grow your wounds.

Say it more ardently—
Suffer your soul
to become my comfort
and I'll worry hurry
till your arms are home.

Say it with a stutter—
I spend my strength
spelling out s-p-i-d-e-r
here where it's weather.
We live in the winter.

    Say it in letters.

You peel my crayons.
Please, it's a pleasure.
Say it sincerely—

    I can be friends.

Frank Made This Up for Us

Sing this song of cards and crowds.
Sing this song of playing.
Sing this song for dames and deals.
It's luck and losers singing.

Sing this song for hearts and bars.
Keep the lovers living.
Sing this song and deal some more.
Don't let your voice get whiny.

Sing this song just once for me.
Sing it like you mean it.
I know you cheat—I can read.
Just sing and don't explain it.

The Last We Ever Heard from Eugene She Said—

Here I am so
walk me toward something mad and moony, like
the color of crescents splitting blood from the clouds.
Tell me something. Tell me that we're each
maid and man in our horrors and in our halls of cloth.
Open me like a melon and with both your hands
eat out the sweet wet heart of my very arms and head.

Toward something sad and lonely, I see
all the bright edged arrows blinking. Time drives by.
In the night life thickens and I hear
the very earth and air pleading as if it too felt the fear.
Caught in vines of fire and veins, I want both
your hands to walk me down this path of flesh and water.

Full Moon through the Veranda Door

I'll Meet You Tonight

I'll meet you tonight
when the stars are sparklin' bright
and the moon is just a sailboat on the river.
I'll bring the wine.
You bring lots of time.
And we'll speak soft and low with each
                                                    other.

The nights have been so warm.
You can lean against my arm
and toss a nickel at that big ol' catfish.
Or maybe just for fun
we'll swim out and give him one
and in return he'll grant us what we both
                                                    wish.

Oh, I'll wish you near me,
hourly and yearly.
I'll hug you close and you'll go, "mm, me
                                                  too."
Then Catfish, he's goin' to say.
"Yez suh, I got away,
and I got a way to make your wish come
                                                  true."

Just meet me tonight
when the stars are sparklin' bright
and the moon is just a puddle on the water.
I'll bring the wine.
You bring lots of time.
And we'll speak soft and low.
And we may get to know one another.

A Face of Excitement

FIRST THERE WAS AN OILWELL PLOWING THE FIELD,
THEN EVERYBODY WAS RIDING ON THEIR TRACTOR.
FINALLY, THE GROUND WAS READY TO ME MEAT.
THE DUST JUST KEEPS GROWING HIGHER EVERY DAY.
WE WENT OUT TO CHOP WEEDS AND LOST OUR FEET.
EVEN HIRED HANDS CLOSE TO DRY SWEAT & ITCHES.
GOD, HAYFEVER AND BRUSH SCRATCHED AT THE SKY.
"TAKE THINGS YOU SHOULD BE ABLE TO SEE THROUGH,"
FRANK TOLD DIRK. "LIKE, FOR INSTANCE, YOUR EYES,
IN THIS WEATHER THEY RUB ON THE PINK OF PAIN."
FLOW SAID SHE HAD A CASE OF COLA LAST NIGHT.
SHE WAS TELLING FRANK IT WAS THE 24HR VARIETY.
FINALLY, THE MEAT WAS READY TO BE GROUND.
CAN'T SAY NO ONE ASKED ME FOR MORE FUROR,
THOUGH DIRK WAS ONE WHO COULD APPROXIMATE.
GOD, THE SHADOWS OF HIS EYES WERE JUST FAMOUS.
THEY EXACTLY MATCHED THE SIZE OF TWO WINDOWS.
IN THEM A PALOMINO AND A BURNT BAY GLANCE BY.
BUT THEN THERE WERE TRENCHERS ABOUT THE FARM.
THE FARMERS KEEP TIGHT FIELDS AND DRY FURROWS.
LAST TIME IT RAINED FLOW CAUGHT A COLD OF WATER.
THERE ARE FOUR (4) QUARTS OF WATER ON THE PORCH.
THEY MOLD ON THE OLD STOVE BY THE KITCHEN STEP.
THE RAIN CAME YELLOW AND PINK IN PUDDLES, BUT
YOU CAN'T GRAB RELIEF OUTBACK IN A SMOKEHOUSE.
THE TARANTULAS TRAVEL AND DISTRACT A PURPOSE,
EVEN ONE AS IMPORTANT AS TEARING OFF A SCAB.

THAT WAS WHY FRANK LEFT DIRK AND ME OUT OF IT.
WE COULDN'T GET THE TACK ROOM UNLOCKED.
SO, I DECIDED I'D BE LONELY AND SCHIZOPHRENIC.
CAN ANYONE ACTUALLY GET BACK TO THEIR BROTHER?
DIRK GAVE ME A FACE OF HIS MOMENTARY EXCITEMENT.
HE DREW IT OUT ON A LARGE SHEET OF CARDBOARD.
IT WAS ROUND AND OLD LIKE THE TOP OF A HATBOX.
FLOW AND VI HAD ALREADY GONE TO THE
` MEETING GROUNDS.
TWO YOUNGER GUYS CAME BY—
         ASKED IF FRANK'D BEEN ROUND.
SHIT, I SHOWED 'EM DIRK'S NEW
                       RAW LEATHER HEADBAND.

Good Lookin'

Handsome is as handsome does.
    Handsome says his hands are cold.

Hell, tell Handsome wear some gloves.
    Handsome's young sez ugly's old.

Handsome sez as Handsomes told.
    Never thought he'd fall in love.

Not with someone he couldn't hold.
    Handsome certainly has his woes.

He found his hands on the stove.
    Now how will he ever shove?

Handsome is and likes to move
but only shows what he means to lose.
    —Cripple and Jake

Weird Clouds

    RAILROAD
    FOOL MOON
    BROKEN GLASS
    KITTY CAT
    TWO OF US
    NO MATCHES
    BURNT MUS-
        TACHES
    EAR TO RAIL
    NO TRAIN
     NO RAIN
    FOR ONCE
WHO ARE YOU?

Fortune Cookie
You will be successful in love.

Dick at work.

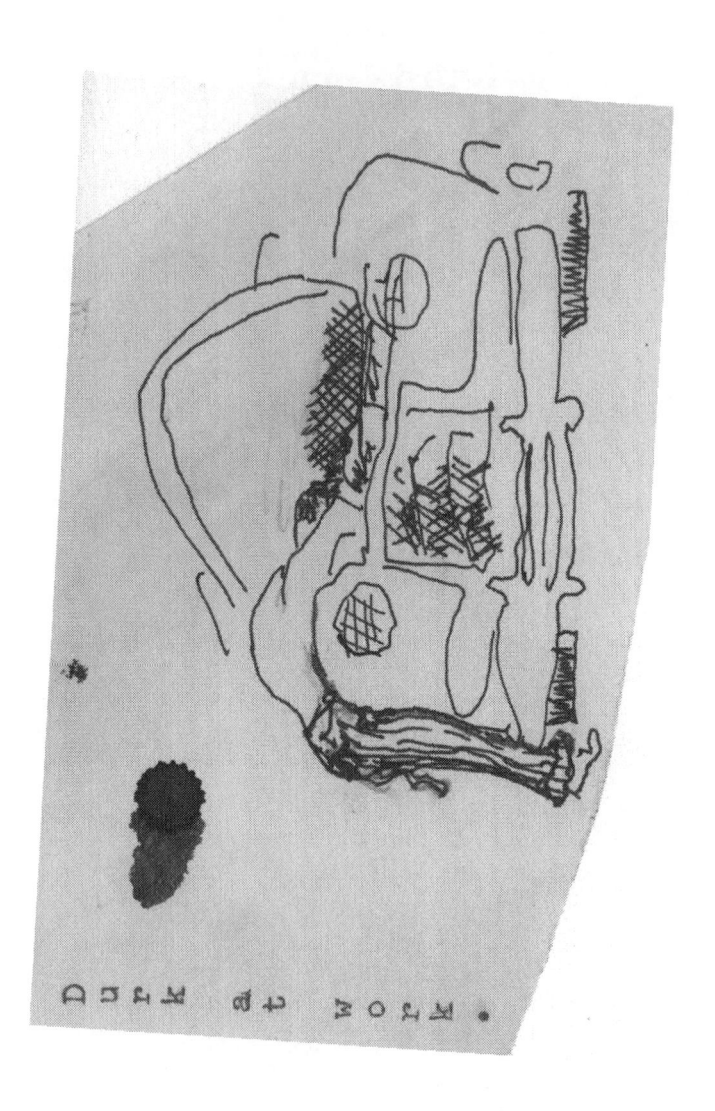

It's Tough Being Tough

Like Boots, the long windows
have come and gone. I never
thought he was joking. Neither
did Foster or Vivian. The day
comes—the windows get up an're
long gone. I remember us washin'
them.

Now, Boots did do most the labor.
But I helped. I hung'em out on the
line, and I'll not soon forget
watchin' the magenta sunset that
evenin'. Or how…or how the last
bits of sun showed through the clean
wet glass of the long windows.

    Boots
was going soon. We all felt that near.
The night first long window got
busted, I suppose that's the night
I first suspected. And then later
there was his letter. Oh, Vivian
broke down at the edge of a tear.

Tore up the letter—"He wants t'
break it off." She sobbed. Chet seen
him bundling up his old green Chevvy.
That was something—we all know it
now. Vivian just shook. She shook
her whole body, and she shook her
head. She said, "it's pulled and
dark as curtains—oh, I wish I'd
be a widow. Foss? Jole? What am I t'
make of it?" They comforted her
on the shoulders. I sat on the porch.
"There, there." I'd hear Jole say.

Boots…Boots? We knew Boots'd
not be seen, not even far off—
like the palomino or the burnt bay
in the majesty of the long windows.
Or seen the way he was
                              ever again.

Of the Author
(photo by Mike Mullin)

Photo by Mike Mullin

We put ourselves together
so many different ways,
but we all come apart
just the same.
—Larry Gene

Book Two

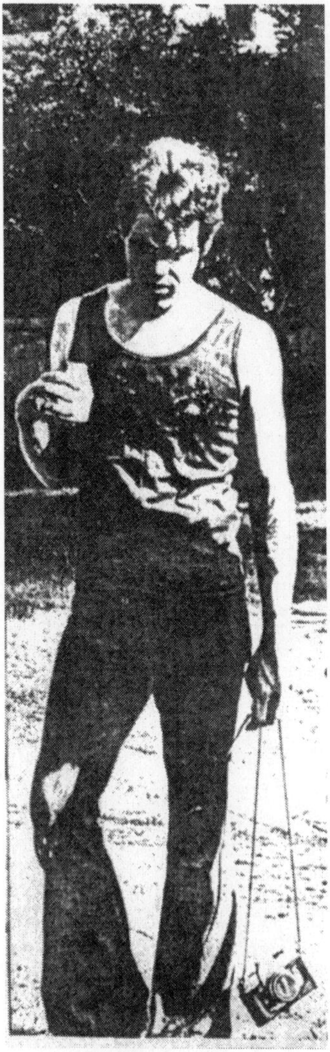

So Long
Long
– ing
Goes
On

"Longing accomplishes all things."
—Mary Renault

DearHon

typin' by candlelight
dringking givenBeer
listen to 54's 45s
just like I always
wanted or imagined so

lots ofLove to yours

   just imagine …

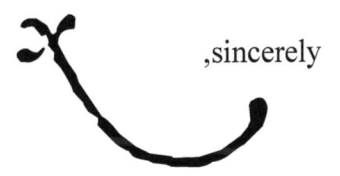

,sincerely

So Longing Goes On
© copyright 1977 by Larry G. Bierman

"LIFE TO YOU IS JUST A BOOK."
—Lindy Kyle Teague

I am Fire
You are Heaven
You are Ch'ien
I am Lie
  below or
  above me
Change is fortune
  and love yours

kiss you, angel

Burgers In Bed
(Opal & Blue)

Heart Jewels

Ripped this out
in the glare
of the night.

Wrote it out
in the death
of a quiet.

I could see
by the two
of your eyes,

> you were lonely
> in the core
> of a week.
>
> Featured it
> —just so—
> at the sheets.
>
> Tore my soul
> from inside
> my sneakers.
>
> Held it like you.
> Loved you.
> And you let go.

```
OPAL
THOT
AND
CHAN
GED
 HER
MIND
```

Missing Part

I dipped inside myself this morning
my boots on the desk so attractively,
    in them sleepy toes

I had a few Polaroid's I wanted to take:
you, the aquarium, Christmas light—
    I thought about nature a lot

I smelled a rose in the snow and shivered.
In icicle memories of your importance
    I came across a missing part.

Breakfast News

there's been this death
in the family
and the newspaper didn't
get it straight

the death was sudden—
people talk about it
and are wrong

Carl's Vietnam Death

   not all that patriotic
        but the other day
    the flags flapping
through the long-needle pine
  high above the redbud
     moved me a little

   even though those flags
have been politically misused
        i was reminded
  (a mutual friend told me)
     though Carl was not
  all that patriotic—
        not even brave

    through the pines
   the flags merrily
     (innocently)
       flew

and the tulips grew—
     and the tulips grew

**SO LONGING GOES ON
LONGING GOES ON SO
ING GOES ON SOLONG
GOES ON SO LONGING
ON SO LONGING GOES
SO LONGING GOES ON
LONGING GOES ON SO
ING GOES ON SOLONG**

Reincarnate

      Return,
If there are not storms,
and I will get to hold
you…
      I must let you go.

Mountains in my arms,
      I will live here.
And
when you've done,
    you can find me
by the lines
  in the sky.

      There is no end…

AM–FM

not much
 bad as
 i know
 feel it
 get kissin'
   hot
 also
  drunk
    pushy
whistling
some 're suns
  radio gas
  station
 pumps

A Headband Construction

Now working
 on local-color,
in the middle of
a headband construction,
we have blue&yellow
 beads

Journal Entry

Judges run amuck.
Convicts die.
Our civilized age.
A child is drawn out.
Now he draws…
We open flowers.
 "Petals lost."

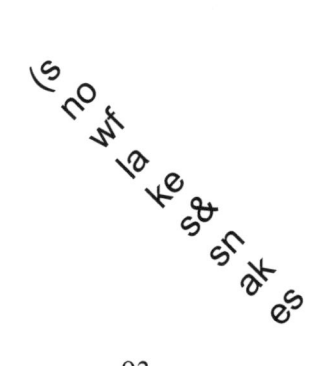

(snowflakes&snakes)

Let a Lot

Let a lot./Let a lot./ Let a lot.
Let me place the face across the room,
the electric space the time drams erased,
and voices that populate the thought…
Let me try again to make myself thin/kind
of like the pin you keep torturing toward
your tenuous film…Let me touch your
knees and plead. And please, please, let me
leave when you've no more need for me…
Let me escape death's hallucination with
no hurt./Let me forget spit and hints./Let
an empty room fill with moonlight and a
vacant bed be no reason for regret.

Long Long Haul

1) This is not the mountain.
    This is not the snow.
    Though these look like tracks
        and it is cold,
    it is too cold
        for this to be snow

2) We were warm,
        but this is another season.
            You are not that close.
            You are not that close.
        I have to wear more clothes.
        It is the season of ice.

3) This is not the mountain.
    There's nothing here to climb.
        This is a page and writing,
    and though it has been walked on
    it still is not the road.
    This is not the snow.

4)   —What I mean is—
        this is what I wrote.
    This is what I wrote
        when I wanted you.
    I wanted you to know
        that this is not the mountain,
    and that I can live with ice.
        I can try to live with ice.

Innocent So

The capacities of love scare me…
& think we might actually
have…scares me silly…the
capacity of loves.

Wow

remember the lady who bought a king-size bag of potato chips just to have something comfortable to sit on?

Tulsa Speedway:
4th of July & Z Z Top

"MAN , I JUST GOT
J. GILES' DRUMSTICKS
& I FEEL GREAT!!!!"
    ALL HELL-RAISERS
    CLOSE SHAVERS
    LIFESAVORS
    SPORTS MAJORS
    & BEARDS TURNED LOOSE

SLIM SAILORS
LITTLE LABORERS
& THE NEIGHBORS
GIVE BIG FAVORS
& CANS OF CRAZY JUICE

      —CABRON—

    ALL HELL-RAZORS
    LEATHER BLAZERS
    BOLD BEHAVIORS
    AND SPANISH OATHS—
    SEE WHO'S GOT GUT

LIFE

DOESN'T GO

No Joke, Joe

after you scrape the ice off
the shield, after you realize
the glass is scratched bad,
after you get in the car and
the handle falls off in your
hand, after you wait in line
for a long time, you know no-
where to leave

after you've left your lunch
half eaten, changed the radio sta-
tions a dozen times, played
for big stakes and reset the
clock, you know the time won't
make a bit of difference

Buffalo, Oklahoma

Walked out beyond town—
    turned down
the broad arroyo
and watched the sun.
And watched the sunset.

Kneeled in the sand
    and sang—ah.
Put a rock in my pocket
and listened to desert larks
break the closing dark.

Wished on the jets
    I saw.
My wish was power—
wished love. That's all—
peace, love and rainfall.

Braniff–Flight 980

The ground is down and brown
all around between the wing
and the motor.
Half awake, have a Coke
in my hands
and the glittering South Canadian
                     in sight.
It's been years since I've been
       14,000 feet high.
Mostly I've walked the same
  six square blocks, but I believe
you'll find me. We will meet.
       I believe.

Longing

Opal pulls on
her stars blouse.

Her hands move
 like photographs.

Veined glass
and windows prism
where Opal's lashes
⠀⠀⠀⠀⠀catch a tear.

And
⠀⠀⠀candles
⠀⠀⠀⠀⠀⠀burn
⠀⠀⠀⠀⠀⠀⠀⠀⠀vanilla.

Look Up Words

The sentence flows simple as
whirlpools from pinwheels,
as breathing and phantoms.
My head leaks water, dear Barbara,
at the thought of your blues and
waters rush every river to seas.
These nerves learn love
         in the strange dawn
of the dictionary's revival.

6:45 Arrival

The windows are shut—
the curtains hang open,
pulled from the walls.

The moon polished out nails.

LT's warm,
almost handsome.
We go to the mountains.
He says tomorrow we'll
        go to the mountains.

CONE

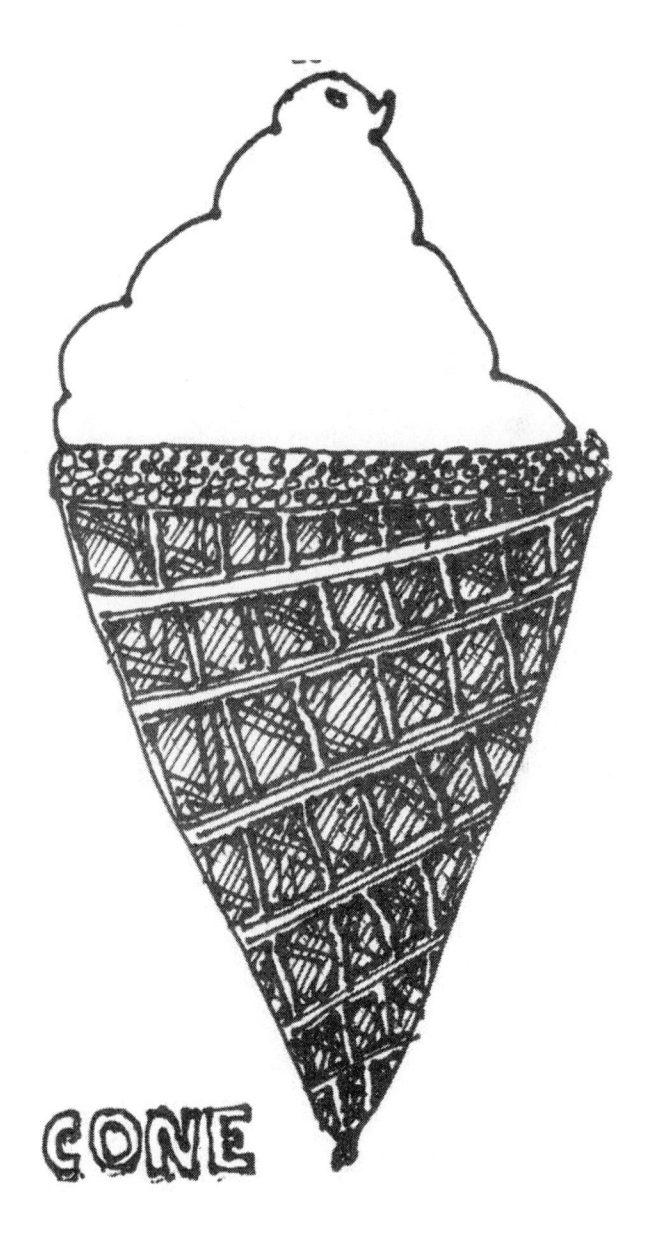

Snowman*in*Moonlight

Ten perfect snowflakes
  gather on the petals
    of a pure white sky.
    It's good
building a fire.
    The air gets starker
      as a strong man takes
        to the slope.
Plumes glisten
  as nice
    as he veers.

Appeal

Say, damn,
on my knees.

    Just let me
    live in heaven.

Power Glide
(for Karen Silkwood)

on the air
in our water
underground
open lips
fly the freeway

           in rivers
           and flesh
         spurts of fluid
        block the bypass
       tons of aluminum

hard bargains
over atoms
toward OKC
safe & swift
to the ground

Standing Looking

The back door's open.
The trees are growing.
It seems like winter,
but it isn't snowing.

HELL

!

HAV
E Y
OU
GOT
A
MAT
CH?

EAT—YOUR $

   Spent a
   whole
   book of
      matches

   and still
      no glow.

Drawing to Color

(Denver, Colorado)

want/to want

First lessons in Food & Drink

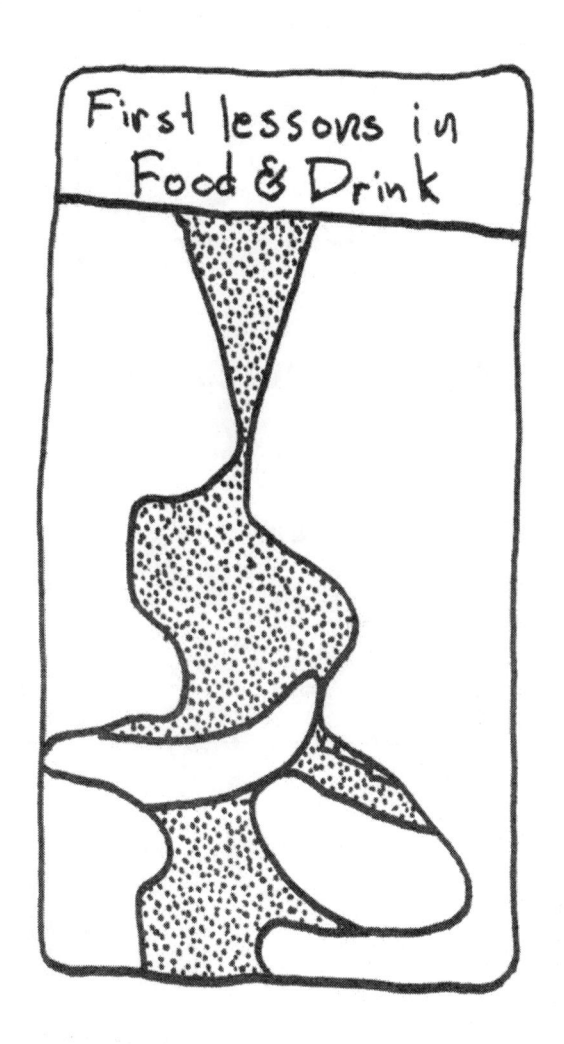

Meditate

I lick my gums.
I check my socks
  with my thumbs.
I have a box.
My temples drum.

Ponca City Birth

I am a woman.
I shall fold
my butterflies
into fists
    as I clutch
    at the light.
I shall flood
scarlet onyx
like scarves
at my wrists.
    I shall shed.

Light above Table

Five men stand
  brown hair and blond.
Two men seated
  sun-blond and well cut.
Two play backgammon.
  All drink Michelob.

Joe comes in from the cold.
He's been throwing balls
              for the dog.

The mountain light slants
  constantly through glass,
through the smoky air,
  across the sofa, arms, rug.

NOTHING VAGUE ABOUT INSINUATION

Six on the Last Straw

    6 of us with lighters
    sit religious as gulls,
    hushed and not blinking.
    We watch bridges give way.
    The flames shoot blue
              as blood.
    Around an agate, 6 of us
    burn our belongings
        in order to keep cool
    at the End-of-the-World.

A VAST FORCE IS OUT TO DESTROY THIS WORK

Dropping like Flies

Sunstroke on the mezzanine.
Heart attack on Fifth and Walker.
Slit throat along Canal Street.
Electrocution in the bathroom.
Poisoned in the kitchen.
Asphyxiated in the garage.
Shot to death in pajamas.
Drowned in the kiddy pool.
Run over by a garbage truck.
Complications of a flesh wound.
Old age in the early morning.
After years of serious illness.
Snakebite by the campfire.
Broken neck while water-skiing.
While driving down a train track.
Asleep in a dumpster.
Love to the wrong woman.
From a low-flying plane.
Overboard in the Caribbean.
After the Saturday night fight.
Alone in a porch swing.
Smothered under plastic.
Choked on beef liver.

Flown the Coop

(Why did the chicken…?)

Last Will

    If you own your own farm
you should always keep a good
gentle cow, and raise feed
and have some truck patches,
and store your own feed, and
put up hay, have some livestock,
several head of cattle and some
pigs, and a bunch of chickens,
and take care of your livestock,
and sell off the increase of your
stock when it will top market prices.
    You can farm eighty acres by
yourself with nothing but a team
of horses. I've done it myself
many times—of course my sisters
would come by once in awhile and
put the house in shape and help
me with the canning.
    When I was young we'd can in
half-gallon jars, and there was
enough of us that it would be
pretty well eaten in a day.
    Big yellow corn is good for
horses and pigs—and mix in
a little buttermilk with the slop.
    I grew that potato you've been
peeling—morning, noon and night.

Dance by Yourself

Take a mad spin on the toe.
Throw your arms in the air.
    Share your features—
joy, pain, love and longing.
Come to a stage
    as if it would never end.
Reach out and leap.
  Bend your fingers.
    Let your toes touch.
Both hands overhead,
  tie ribbons in the air.
Roll on the floor.
  Make the stars dizzy.
    Run in spirals and twirl.
  Flower with your body.
Be a cobra in the bushes.
  Jump through a hoop sky.
  Make rain and snow.

Your eyes lead the hand.
Every move is your first.
Give into and then create…
    tension.

On the toe.
    Spin and hold—

For Christy
(when we were Flower Children)

Christy in her basement moves
at the window, naked in the morning
as I am where I stand.
I can see her body supple
in garments of ivy at the window
and shining in the dawn.

In the daytime Christy works
to earn her living selling pipes and
papers in a shop uptown.
Smiling through bead doorways
at the people on the pavement
in her bells and feathers,
hear her turn around.

And in the evening she calls
me down her stairway and talks
to me in Spanish of a secret
treasure she…she keeps.
She is a kind of pouring rain
upon the forest teaching me
the movement of love and of
                              cosmic peace.

Dark inside her feels dark
inside the night quiet high
inside our dreaming hearts
we sleep soundly,
till Christy in her slippers
opens up her shutters, shivering
in the morning. Oh, we stretch,
laughing yawn.

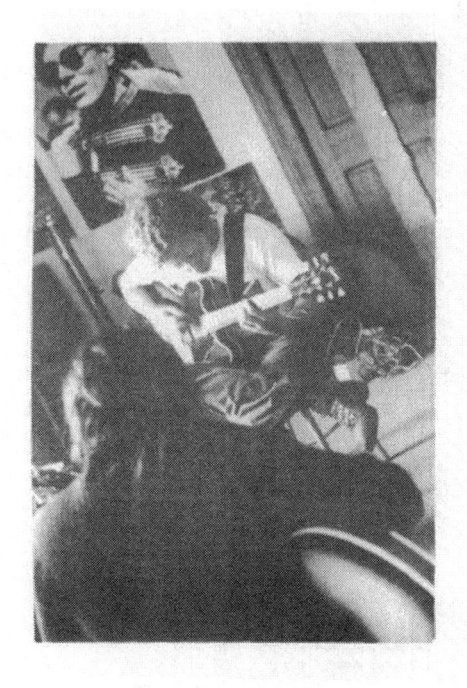

Guitar Music

(Blue & Joe)

Showed *(for Nick Sunday)*

Could / see you out.
Could see / you to the door.
Could see you / before you go
and I don't see you—
    no, no more.
      You / showed me things.
      You showed / & it was grand.
      You showed me / how to sing.
      Made me feel
          one of the band.
Can / hear you now.
Can hear / you on the road.
Can hear you / in a crowd
playing out loud
    above the roar.
      You showed / showed me things.
      You showed / me my own hands.
      You showed me / how to sing.
      Made me feel
          one of the band.
Will / see you through.
Will see / you in my eyes.
Will see you / as you see me.
Oh, we're so
        recognized.

Is Your Soul Worth 25¢?

I've been cleaning and cleaning.
I vacuumed the corners and couch,
vacuumed the popcorn out of my boots,
washed the smudges off the door,
cleaned the light bulbs and shades,
    (now I can see!)
wiped off all the spice bottles,
shook the rug and beat the bed,
damp wiped all the piano keys,
took my tie to the cleaners,
blanched some rice, brushed the lintels,
sanded the cat box, shined the mirrors,
re-stacked the magazines (by date),
and emptied the vacuum.
I soaked the drapes in Downey,
used Mr. Clean on the shower curtain,
removed the bathtub ring,
polished the pots, pans and lids,
swept the hall, sponged the rail,
rinsed the garbage cans,
dusted the cactus,
vinegared the candelabra,
Spic'n'Spanned the rocker,
sudsed the cellar,
and polished the flower planters
    beautifully green.
Tomorrow I'll air out the attic
      and rearrange my past.

Hold Up

For four lonely nights
I've listened in Denver.
I've watched local news
    and colored my blues.

> *Kiss my mouth.*
> *Steal my cover.*
> *Buy my act.*
> *Be my lover.*

For four lonely nights
I've haunted the winter.
I've waited for your word
    and felt of my bruise.

        (If it weren't for Crayolas
        and Braniff I'd've killed myself
        a long time ago. Yes.)

"Who's been blotting their lipstick om y briefs?"

Got KICKED OUT OF
school so NOW I'M IN
THE PARK WORKING MY NAME
IN THIS BENCH —
MY HEART'S ♡ SO SORE!
I SPENT THE AFTERNOON
ON THE FLOOR MAKING MY
HANDS INTO FISTS —
IF I HAVE TO STAY OUT
I MAY GO ALL THE WAY
AWAY...
GOING NOW INCH BY INCH —

NO MATTER WHAT I WILL BE AT THE DANCE!

Watched the Marquee Change

SQUIRM is
  now showing
    at the movie.
The fat kid
  who sells
    popcorn
climbed up
  the step
    ladder
      & spelled out
the COMING
  ATTRACTION.
"A night of
      crawling terror!"
starts tomorrow.
    For now
  I'll have to
make do.

@
Just sniffed seventeen sheets
of pink and cream pornography.
I keep wondering what if—

RELAX-IT
(RM #60)

*COWS MOO 'ROUND THE NEW KING MOTEL*AND THE PHONE'S FOR ONE ROOM OVER*EACH COLOR TV COMES ON AUTOMATICALLY*THE SHOWER HAS NO PRESSURE BUT'S HOT*PIGS RUN THROUGH THE THICK FOG AND COUGH*FOOD COMES IN HUGE EXPENSIVE QUANTITIES*RUBBER BANDS HANG OUT OF PAPERBOY POCKETS* AT THE TG&Y BETH HAS ON HER KISS SWEATER*HER EYES'RE CROSSED BUT SHE'Z CUTE*SHE SAYS KISS IS ONE OF HER FAVORITES, TOO*TOMORROW THE PLAY GOES ON & ONLY THE BUTLTER KNOW HIS PART*COWS MOVE AROUND AND MOO IN THE MIST*ALL NIGHT LONG OUTSIDE THE THIN MOTEL WALLS*SCRAPE SEQUINED ICE OFF THE WINDSHIELD*MAKE SURE THOSE COWS MOO-VE OVER***

Tag

Remember the time we wrote
our names on the overpass—
our initials on the water tower—
   EUNICE & SLIM
just like that—on the fence
 around the drive-in?

With your purple ballpoint pen
you wrote your name on my arm.
I wrote my name on the knee
of your jeans and drew hearts
on the bottoms of your feet.

     Remember—
        it was too hot
            for boots?

Wonder Why Wonder

in the winter. Feel it getting dark.
It's so black that earth and air tremble,
then crawl over my body all night long.
Youth grows in grass like a golden wound;
I hold you in my arms and you bleed—
dark oozes through the windows like fog
and like very tender snow falls over us.

THICK COVERS ON THE LAMP

LION ONBLACK VELVETABOVE THE COLOR TV
BIGBLACK PILLOWIN THECENTER'F THEROOM
A PHONEBY THE COFFEE TABLEON THEFLOOR
THE WOVENICE CANESTER THEJIM BEAMBOTTLES
THEDOG ANDLOTS OF RUGS * STARTREK ON THE
TUBE PILESOF VIVEANDPEOPLE UNDER THEDESK
HANDSON THEPIANO BENCH * CIRCULARBAR IN
THECORNER A WHITEBEAR SKINRUG SHOWSTEETH
ATTHE HEADOF THEBED TABLES OFSTATUES
I/AM/BEING OWNED * AGRAND DEMANDS BLUES
BARBARA MUSTTALK * BARABARAMUST TALK
LIONON BLAQVELEBET ABOVETHE MEXICANRUGS

Drinks

Break the ice and pass me a slice.

Camp Night–Meet

No clearing! Let's burn
the church. We sit around
the blaze and sing pop songs.
             The choir joins in.
The wood works great—
    goes up in 100 ft shafts.
Last week we burned the school.
Billows of black and yellow
    tumble and vanish from the
beautiful memorial windows.
             Long windows.
We try to remember—
    how old is Neal Young?
We try but can't really think
               of anything.
What everyone else thinks?
We sing it out loud
and teach it to each other
     like a broken law
             we got fixed.

Durant Tour

    She lives in *Le Chateau.*
I met her across from the Cricket Box.
She stood by a marble column looking very
expensive in white. (She smiled at me.)
        We met & went for a stroll.
Together we watched a puppy in the creek.
We saw a purple football by the pears,
    a rocker-recliner in the alley,
        and an Indian in the sunset.
We saw an old man and a young man
load a handmade baby bed
into the back of a new Ford pickup.
The house across from the high school
    had a grin in its awning and
        an air-conditioner in its eye.
A girl jumped trampoline on Evergreen Street.
We saw a spider web big as all the four o'clocks.
A church was letting out and we saw
the same person drive by in two different cars.
There was a lawn of gigantic zinnias.
A pink football team posed
        in the camera store window
while the smell of fresh buttered popcorn
           wafted out of the movie.
In the parking lot a young tough smoked
    a cigarette like a life-time habit he didn't
      quite have yet.
           We walked forever.
Funny, she didn't seem like he type.

mi-
my last
. Another in
le of where my la
nded. And another mess
heart to star-crossed hea
is one. Have lots of fun. Get s
on the run. Get set. Ready. Run! So
d come. Isn't it fine here? Don't you mi
her have grass any old night. But you walk on
all over me. What's that supposed to feel like
ou it hurts like hell. How can you forget? Lets
it's the other night. Remember what? I want a s
serious business. If we don't keep in touch. O,
ll just up and die. Who wants to remember? Somet
so hard I get choked up and I cry. But that's s
ool's story. I'm not going to write it. I live w
sts and Unitarians. I don't believe much, but the
nd. If you think about it there is a mind. That'
nt. I think I'll just fall over dead some day. Th
s are the tastiest part. How little I expect from
ou are all I've got. Another in the very middle o
y last letter left. It took all my heart. I bend
o the center and sing. Hold me, or anything. Why
night like tonight? Where's my drink? You're a s
you're a saint. And that's about all I can say.
feel of you. Don't feel of me. I want to be wit
ime I look you leave. I give you gallons and gal
eaded gas. Sit in your worry. I dream of your fol
your dancing feet, the folds in your wonderful b
ork. Don't worry. So glad you could come. Here w
sn't it a sun. I'm going under. The telephone's
rong number. The edges of the problems get fuzzy.
really mean for me. How long have we been trying
ng? I wonder and it thunders. We don't get any y
me you system. I want to be part of it. I want a
everything fits. I expect so very little of you.
n't you remember them? They pointed us out in th
ime it was so dark. The dogs ran after us. I wai
e cold in the dark on a strange street for five h
you were inside doing a deal, or getting sick. I
ry. I pounded my fists on the dash and clinched
ll they hurt. I needed a coat and a light. You
me about life on the farm. How you rode hor
k down to skinny dip in the pond. How y
ad trucks with hay. Art is the onl
y argued about. Still, this s
the very middle of Americ
e Love left off like
ere wasn't even
a for the ca
you of
tir

Word Workers of the World, Unite!

Cozy

It's been a long time since I slept
in a motel where the pillows
    are rolled like quarters.
This place was newly redecorated
       in 1958.
I cut my finger with a razor blade just now,
and it bleeds into some toilet tissue.
Went to the Sonic and fell in love again.
I don't know, I'm only going to be in town
less than a week, should I make a date?

That Number 4 with cheese was so cute.
I've got seven and three-quarters hours
to sleep in this seven dollar plus tax room.
Wonder if sleep is worth a dollar an hour?
Take a shower—the personal paper
  bathmat keeps floating
        up around my ankles.
       For a second I passed out
 on this page.
     A loud train
        just shook me awake.

KATT

    walk, walk
    in a time
    for backrooms
      blankets
        on windows
      posters
    on ceiling
      you're so clever

    so's your brother
    (what he rolls
          runs)
      by the stairs
        light cracks
    ice and moss
    in the kitchen

        blackbones
    jazz in the drink
     dirt's own toe
    walk, walk, walk
    TOMM

February

White cat asleep
in your lap,

hmmm, passed out
at the TV set.

Got on your black
& white bowtie.

I like to draw
your…

Of
Coors

Want
to
kiss
you
not
fall
in
this
beer
w
here
all
ther
e is
is
fuzz
—
all
ther
e is
is
fizz.

Hush Up

Turn out the light. Say goodnight. Get real
quiet and turn out the light. Don't think
of drink. Don't get up and get one. Don't
wake a wink. Go to sleep and catch some.
Fold back the sheets. Get a quilt—
you're gonna need one. Fluff the pill-
ow—it's cold and feels numb. Turn out
the light. Close your eye and die till noon.
When we wake up it will still be too soon.

Sonic Drive-in

Hamburger drippin' with mayonnaise.
Tomato seed down the sleeves.
Catsup on the fingers and face.
French fry balance on the knee.

Cup of cola rocks on the dash.
Cigarette smoke comes up from the ashtray.
Hair still wet from the dive and splash
drips on the stereo player and sprays.

Little seed in the cuff and the pocket
got caught in pieces of string and tissue.
The radio plays the same old dumb stuff
about "love" & "leave" & "touch" &
                                        "miss you."

Big lips pressed against the window.
A fist reaches out and grabs the wiper.
An eyeball shines like a polished pinball,
while the carhop acts just like we like her.

Airbrushed Bushes

Nights and days I live with myself—
L. T. wonders what I do with my life—
I explain how I fidget and write.

Cobalt-blue cycles, wheelies and roar—
leather vest of love as much as desire—
L. T. tells me I should take a long ride.

Go Up

'SMOKE
IN UP
GO WORK
HIS SEES
ARSONIST
THE
↓

I See

I keep looking at your arms,
and mean to look in your eyes.

You seem to say, "who cares?"
I keep thinking of your arms.

Tightly Packed Deck

    ACE OF STARS
    FOUR OF SOCKS
    CUT OF CLUBS
    BURN THE DOCKS
    DEUCE OF THUMBS
    QUEEN OF EYES
    PUT DOWN TWINS
    DRAW THE KNIVES
    KNIGHT OF DAWN
    JACK OF FLOWERS
    HANDS OF BLAZE
    SPLIT OF LIPS
    KING OF JOKES
    STICK YOUR STICK—
    NO SNOWS ON JOE

From the Girl that Could not Be to the Little Boy at Sea

Blue says things without regard to fear or means.
What he knows he knows he's not suppose to tell.

Just 'cause you're not paranoid don't mean you're
well. "I feel all of a sudden"—Blue says suddenly.

At the moment this non-returnable bottle seems like
an hourglass—and I'm trying to hold back.

Aside

MAN DON'T SEDUCE ME INTO MAKING YOU GIRL JEALOUS. MAN SAY, THE DEVIL YOU ROOT HIGH

Ginger Lake Lady

Down by the lakeside, hold my hand.
Picking up the driftwood—rolling
in the sand—wading in our underwear—
talking two alone—listen to the croak-
ing of the bullfrog moan.
    Ginger Lake Lady, come and ride in my
    canoe. I got a song—I want to do it
    just for you. Ginger Lake Lady, can I
    take you in my car? 'Cause I want to play
    my song for you on my Nipponese guitar.

Sitting on the riverbank, skipping a
stone—sipping on a cola can—hey,
don't go home. Come to the boat dock,
second on the right. There'll be a party
there, baby, tonight.
    Well, everything's fine. Yeah, and it's
    all swell. I sold a fish—got a three-
    dollar bill. Got me some wine where the
    moonshines still. And I'm going to feel
    finer. Oh, you know I will.

Ginger Lake Lady, come and ride in my
canoe. I got a song—I want to do it
just for you. Ginger Lake Lady, can I
ride you in my car? 'Cause I want to play
my song for you on that Japanese guitar.
                    (It's a Yamaha!)

Mutt Street

Sit in a sprinkle on Mutt Street.
Got nothing to do but sit on my seat.
Hunt for the fleas in this humid heat.
I sit around and drink 'cause there's
                nothing to eat.

Mutt Street—Mutt Street,
mud and ruts on Mutt Street,
fall in a hole and lose your soul,
'cause it's all downhill on Mutt Street.

You're 'pposed to have a tag on
                Mutt Street.
It helps to have a nose, tail and four feet.
All's in the bowl's old bones sans meat,
but you don't have to worry about
                    being neat on

Mutt Street—Mutt Street.
Pups and guts on Mutt Street,
fall in a ditch and lose your bitch,
'cause it's all downhill on what street?
        It's all downhill on that street!
        It's all downhill on Mutt Street.

Glib Future

Bookcases stood up against the wall.
Lovers from Texas relaxed with black hair.
They found the car abandoned in Duncan.
Blood was on the seat, but not human blood.
Someone had tortured a large dog to death.
The animal was repeatedly stabbed and hacked
with part of one of the windshield wipers.

Being short was now very fashionable.
Ladies began wearing horizontal stripes
and spent hours touring the azalea garden.
Texans began taking sugar with their tea.
No one could keep the weekdays straight.
Game shows were big on prime time TV.
No longer were kids satisfied with marijuana.
Preachers began preaching the Song of Solomon.
Huge numbers of people worried about whales.
All the stars shone bluer and bluer than ever.
No one could see anything without illustrations.

Grandparents maimed themselves for attention.
The government had more power than ever,
but power was no longer able to keep control.

The doors continually stuck in their jams.

I'm Your Slave, Joe

Let's get away a way.
Know a way to go.
We'll go in style.
Go all the way? Yo,
bro …cannot stay.
Noone's on blue waves.
Play for the sky.

The Grapes

Slick boy, slim
with purple guitar
say he don't want
to be no rock star.

There're other men in her life

2:00AM on the Band Bus

It's hard coming out of the dreams of
the ice machines, the buzz saw, the fat woman
with her hand on the faucet part. My face wet,

the bucktoothed thing with the broken nose
jerks its narrow head toward the naked light
and bellows rage off yellow burning pages.

June bugs bite the special bulbs all night.
It's impossible to speculate in such a mess—
the twisted limbs, the rheostat, emergency door.

The curly-haired queen holds her open purse
and blinks at the wreckage from her hysteric,
fun. All the vending machines on Main Street
fall in ruin, while a legend splits on foot.
                                      Storms are worse.

WomanInDarkBrown

Intro

F#m Let me have some
     Before I run
     Get out your gun
     Let me have some
     Pour me some rum
     I got to run
     Blow out that one
     Black out the sun
E   Give me some gum
     Get out your gun
     Let me have some
     I got to run
F#m I got to run
     Let me have some
     Let me have some
     Pour me some rum
     Black out the sun
     Black out the sun
E   Blow out that one
     Boy this is fun
F#m I got to run
     I got to run
     Black out the sun

(fast fade)(the F# minor and the
            E major chords are pounded
            out like machine gun bullets
            hitting the Berlin Wall.)

-146-

Smoke Escapes

In the chair
in the front
of the van
with Ann,

   Randy
   squats
   on a
   toolbox
   in back.

I wonder,
    do cops
     ever stop
parked cars?*

In the fresh
friends are
    fires,
or flowers,

or both.

* Yes.

O

ORANGES & RED LIGHTS REACHES OUT!

You Don't Have to be Broke to Sit on the Curb

The mountains rise and shine.
The sea saws the sun in halves.
Oh, open space feels like heaven,
and blue skies content the eagle.

But I love the excitement of strangers
better than the company of angels.

The room welcomes deep solitude.
The oak woods fill the imagination.
The desert drinks blood and is holy.
The garden breathes perfume and peace.
But I love the traffic, travel with strangers,
better than a heaven full of angels.

I love the activity of cities and strangers
better the multitudes of familiar angels.

STR
ANG
ERS
***
ARE
***
ANG
ELS
***
ANG
ELS
***
ANG
ELS
***
AND
***
LOV
ERS

Suspect

Little knownthe mind
we own—
the breath I take;
your poems by heart!

Best Mistake

>   The crime
>   hides in my
>   mustache.

Favorite Stains

In little spots on the necktie,
near the door, on the brick wall,
along the inseam of white slacks,
on the rug between the piano and
bed, among pages of a photo album,
by the tiger in the picture of Joe,
all over the last letter from him.

Sky Bottle

Get stopped
at the airport.
Need another
leather belt.

Pull a coat.
Twist a top.
Draw a dog,
a boy & hawk.

Draw a girl,
   a fly & pop.

Hobby Boy

Bes' not play anymore with the mo'el
airplane//glue—gunk's all over the room
//everythink're stuck//m'fingerskins peel
prinz//FUNNIES stook on the car-pet// elbows're plastered on the SPORTS//GLOO's
enough to ge' yoo//tho @ 5ft. wingspan//
on your own Nice Day Off…

Pull the Birds off Doorknobs

It's early,
too early to get busy,in a cold
    motel night before dawn
in the hours
    of commuters and
        dreams.

Opal thinks
    by the transistor radio
listening to
    strangeness, reports,

static washes
    through her like a smoke.

She thinks
    about cutting a picture
out
    of last night's paper

but her
    scrapbook burned too.

If You've Loved a Woman, It Hurts

i
get
take
n up
in
feel
ings
&
tang
led
in
arms
eyes

Gone from Us Now

I'm enjoying the postcard
you sent from Paris—
particularly the asexual
image of France.

Blues Mountain

Looked the message
in the spyglass * *
It read like what
was on your lips.
I figured I didn't
have a good idea—
even when the papers
rattled and ripped
and the home gleamed
with nickels and boo…

                Broke a fine glass
              and the Weller's wets
            the Marine harmonica
           as my blood drops
           soak into books—
       the pens and sketches
      (a whole mess of desk)
     are turning Sargasso
with bourbon and bloo…

      Slivers of crystal
      slit my fingertips.
      Pick it all up
     like that waiter did
    in Verdun-sur-Meuse.
      Clean it all up
     like that maitre d'
     in the small café.
   Oh, I do like my foo…

All Guy Said Was

"Wait a minute."
"Say, I'll ride the tiger."
"It's okay."
"No?"
"Uh, that's right."
"I think I can remember
　　　　one thing."
"What was the 3rd, the 3rd
　　　and the 4th album
　　　　we played tonight."
"The names of the 3rd and 4th
　　　albums we played."

Bob kept quiet and threw up.

Leop'ard,

n. a large fierce spotted animal.

I am a leopard
and my spots
are blue.

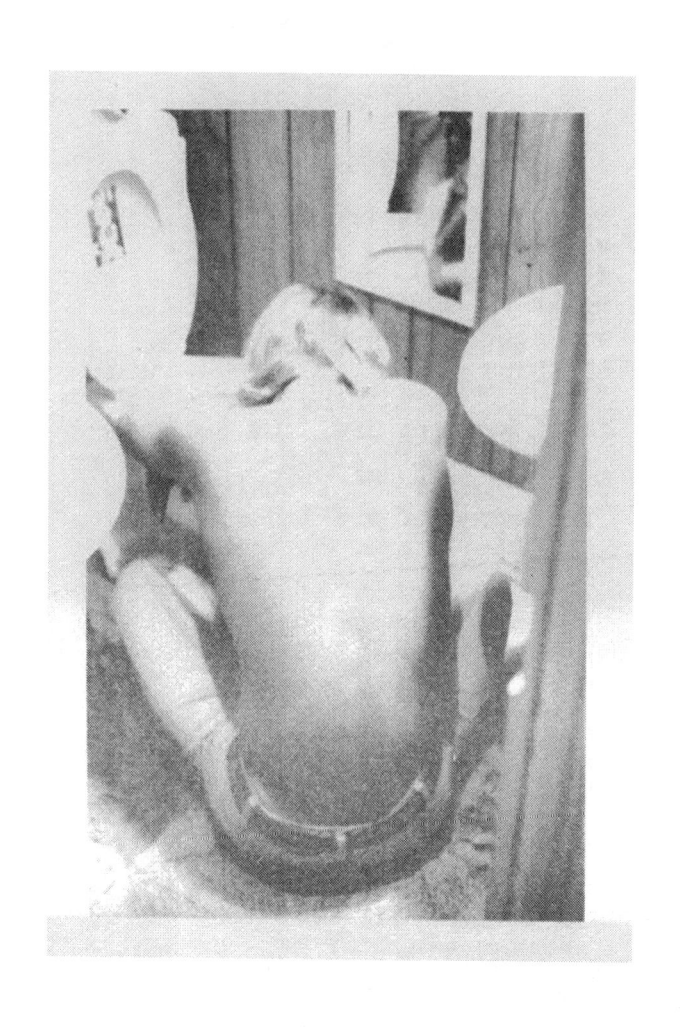

Oh, God.

(Bob)

Bum-a-Stamp

Wrote to Denver.
Want to help
keep my head clear,
clear the air.

Hope that Barbara—
hot to hell—
has her head straight,
'cause I care.

Unknown danger—
my friend's life—
can he take it?
Leave me here…

Certain

Opal's sure Blue loves her—
that's why she gives him no mind.

Not that she wouldn't want to—
she never feels the need.

Soon as Can Be

And when I get
my hands untied,
I mean, get a hand
free—some free
time on hand—
when my time isn't
tied up—I tell
you I'll give you
…I'm just a
　bundle…

Sobre Solo

　Clear,
　frozen
intersection,
　　singing
"Cielito Lindo"
　with hiccups,
　　with tennis
shoes—
　new strings
match the snow.

Romance

In skin the color of pennies,
burned-black nickel eyes
look for ways to spend.

My kids:
 grown up in grace
from house to house
 grown up the same
from mouth to mouth
 grow wild in place
from heart to break
 grow tame, grow on
from land to soil.

At night
 when the light perishes
  long thin fingers
 comb ink-black hair.

Please Me

Please, please me, my bright eyes.
It'll be alright. Hey, there's no need to
cry, babe. I'll treat you so nice.

Please, please me politely. Go
easy. Take a while. Yeah, you're quite a
sight, babe. Please tease me tonight.

Oh, daylight won't notice that
we've been so close as a few jokes and
kisses—that we're close as this.

No, daylight won't know us. Then,
what do we care? Am I asking so
much? Yes/ Then I'll just hold you dear.

please me

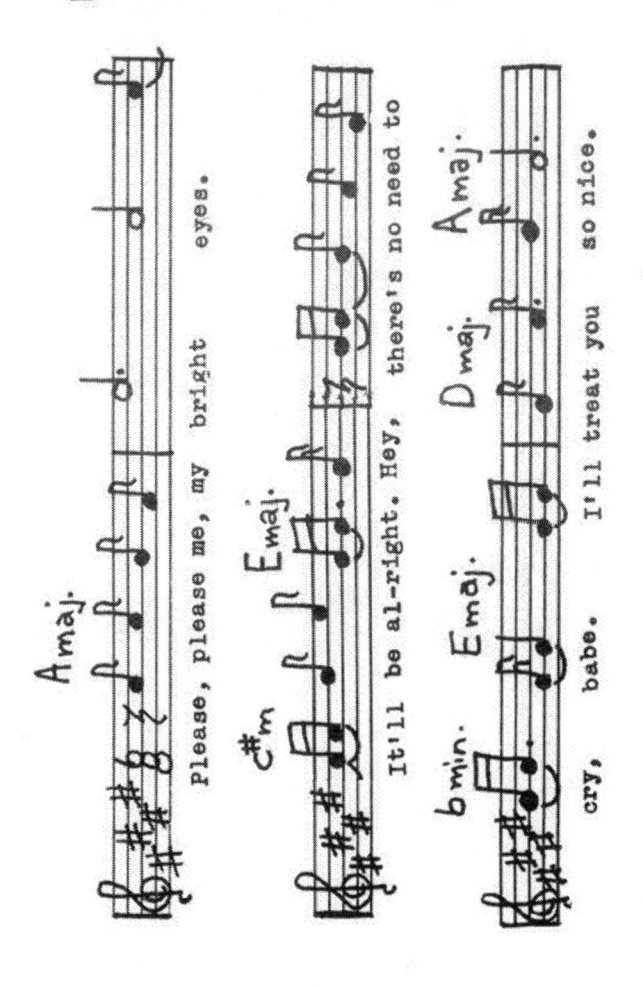

Please, please me, my bright eyes. It'll be al-right. Hey, there's no need to cry, babe. I'll treat you so nice.

BAD DOG

"I'd write a book but I don't have to."

DogDueThanx

this book has
 a big
   dog-dog
    to thank.
Where's my
  other
   black
    shoe?

&TheTreeMadeShade

You let the dawg out --
it's obvious to the town
you didn't keep just dawg
company lastnight . . .
   every success to
      your desires

Detroit Dues—Waltz

Drive my car all night long.
Don't want to go to sleep.
Want to find a girl
  who's big and strong—
let her lift me off my feet.

Drive to the store for a thrill.
Got to get a little to eat.
Want to get a girl who'll
  foot my bill.
You know, I say she's sweet.

Drive my car just 'cause I can—
move it on down the street.
Got to have a girl!
  I'm American, man—
I think girls are neat.

    A few words
           may mean little,
                    but that is all.

Bar Talk

What happened to that speaker—it
looks like the front fell out of it.

She wasn't on the verge of crying,
but she was on the verge of shaking.

The barkeep throws rotten bananas
out the back door into the snow.

Actually a bullet in the gut won't
cause you to fall sideways on the table.

One Name Less

There is no bar.
Your lives just aren't
　that famous.
　　You lost the war—
I don't care what
　you claim is.
　　Where're your senses?
A few answers won't harm—
　might even save us.

Belief to Believe

I'll do anything you'll
  let me.
I'll ride around in your big
  fine car.
I'll compliment you on the size
  of your veins.
I'll buy the kind of drink you
  like best.
I'll let you take all
  the extras.

I'll teach you to play
  the piano.
I'll sit on the bed with you
  and look out the window.
I'll like loud music—I'll like
  loud music.
I'll call everything class
  you want me to.
And I'll always believe
  in what I do.

Hard/Bound

What more can a man ask for
the morning after that night
to remember? The ocher orange
expressionistic landscape hangs
in fuzzy blurs above the bed.
It's time to turn the blanket
off. This is the first time I've
ever slept on a waterbed. It's
time to drink a little orange
juice, fresh squeezed. Is the
fire on? Is it still snowing out?
Hmm? Where did you say you
come from? Me? I'll just stay
out of the way. I'll put myself
over here by this vase of peacock feathers, here by the phone.
Tell me you expect and I'll tell
you when they call. Where are
you going? It's still snowing.
Isn't it? Okay, if you got to get
your car, then you got to get it.
What's it doing over there tho?
The question isn't how can I
face my face. I don't have to
look at my face. The question is

—do I have the guts to show it. Our friends will talk about tonight. And they won't regret what they expect. They said to have fun. This chair seems so proper. I brought a book, just in case. If you want to blow it off, I'll just pass out here in this chair. Do you have a cover for my legs? I don't know— I don't care. It's your first time, but it's not your first time. It just seems like a new, as they say, experience, since you're conscious. It's only a different version of your same old song and dance. Call it a diversion if you like. I take my distraction by the nightstand. They don't call this passion for nothing. Yes. And neither of us is so desperate. We both may look like fools. So? You can hold on as tight as you ever wanted. I'm only here or you can leave. Or, tell me to leave. I don't care. It's all memories to me. And these are your sheets.

Word Worker

In a small
room
at the back
of the house
*Workingman's
Dead*
on the stereo,
thinking
Popov
Vodka & 7up
(happy birth-
day, Chuck),
and driving—
drove Alan
all over
looking
for a dead
dog to beat.

Didn't run
across one.
Walk slow,
Eufaula Street,
to the store.
The neon
sign shines,
"home….."
I'll get to
the finish
of my works,
try to figure
what my
body's worth
around this
mission,
this back
room.
I search
for myself,
put pressure
on the type,
measure
myself—
a life.

Love Poem

Another time.
Blue runway lights/Night.
Holiday lights of Denver.
Full moon on aluminum wing.
A tear in my eye
at the window.   Lindy,
                      my God.
Below—oceans of gray. Cold.
Not even visible mountains.
Just Venus in a black sky.
                  Lindy, live.
                  Lindy, love
        and let me visit you again.

Crying in Braniff roast beef.
175mph tailwind.
A fast trip.
Nothing's left behind me.
You told me to hold your arm.
Like a fool.
I did.
                Live Lindy. Live.
Descent to
    blue lights,
        Will Rogers World—
           Oklahoma City,
                Oklahoma.

Let Me Now

I can be as with you
as without you.

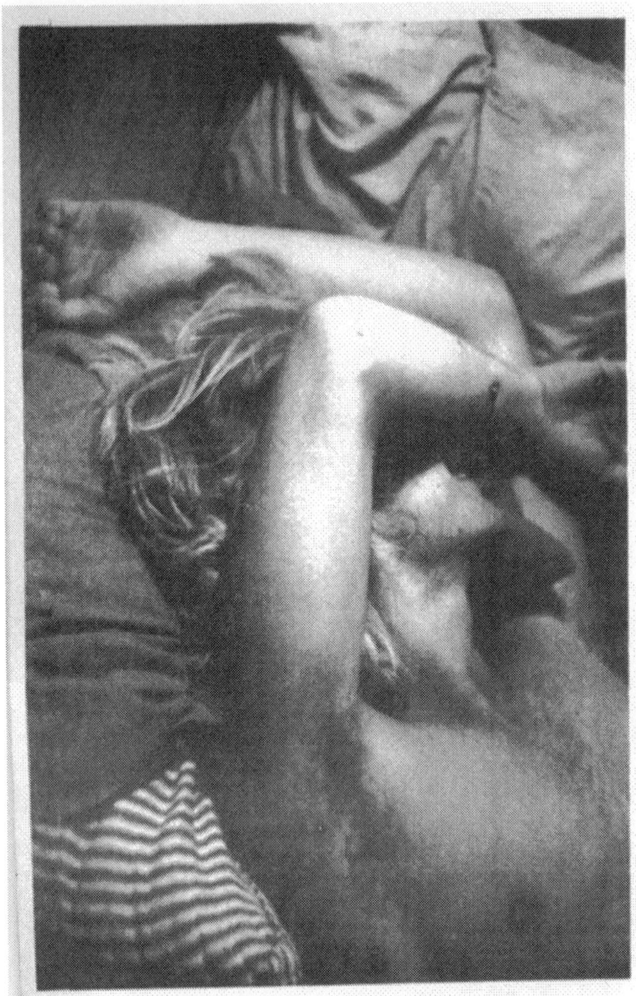

Made in the USA
Charleston, SC
01 December 2010